Dear Diary.The Journey

Prince Sammysam

 pencil

ISBN 978-93-5883-053-8
© Prince Sammysam 2023

Published in India 2023 by Pencil

Contributors:
Editor: Phanuel Ochieng
Editor: Phanuel Ochieng

A brand of
One Point Six Technologies Pvt. Ltd.
Unit no. 26, Ground Floor, Building A1,
Wadala Truck Terminal Road,
Near Post Office, Antop Hill, Mumbai - 400037
E connect@thepencilapp.com
W www.thepencilapp.com

Author biography

Prince Sammysam is a poet with a passion for words and a love for the beauty of language. Born and raised in Kisumu, Kenya.Sammysam has been writing poetry for years, using his words to explore the depth of human emotions and experiences.

Sammysam's poetry is characterized by its raw honesty, vivid imagery, and powerful messages. His work has been published in various literary journals and magazines, and he has performed at poetry events and festivals around the world.

In addition to his poetry, Sammysam is also a upcomingsoftwareengineer. He believes that poetry and art have the power to transform lives and change the world, and he is committed to using his work to make a positive impact on the world around him.

When he's not writing or working, Sammysam can be found watching and playing football or watching movies,exploring new places, and spending time with family and friends. He is always looking for new inspiration and experiences to fuel his writing and creativity.

Follow Sammysam on Instagram/Twitter/ or Text on WhatsApp on +2547420343 to stay up-to-date on his latest poetry and creative projects. Join him on this journey of exploration and discovery, as he uses his words to connect with others and share his passion for poetry with the world.

CONTENTS

Epigraph

"Life is a journey, and if you fall in love with the journey, you will be in love forever." - Peter Hagerty

This quote by Peter Hagerty encapsulates the central theme of "Dear Diary. The Journey" - that life is a journey, with all its ups and downs, and that finding joy in the journey itself is key to living a fulfilling life. The quote speaks to the idea that the experiences we have and the people we meet along the way are what truly matter, and that we should embrace the journey and all that it has to offer. It is a reminder that life is not just about reaching a destination, but about savoring the journey and all the moments that make it worthwhile.

Foreword

"Dear Diary. The Journey" is a beautifully written and deeply personal memoir that takes the reader on a journey of self-discovery, resilience, and growth. From the very first page, the author's voice is clear and authentic, drawing the reader into a world of hopes, dreams, and challenges.

The author's willingness to share their most personal experiences and emotions is a testament to their courage and strength. The diary entries are raw, honest, and unfiltered, providing a window into the author's innermost thoughts and feelings. Yet, despite the often difficult and painful experiences that the author describes, the overall tone of the book is one of hope, optimism, and perseverance.

"Dear Diary. The Journey" is a book that will resonate with readers of all ages and backgrounds. It is a story of the universal human experience - of love, loss, family, and the search for meaning and purpose. It is a reminder that, no matter how difficult life may seem, there is always hope and the possibility of a brighter future.

I am honored to have had the opportunity to read and endorse this book. I have no doubt that it will inspire and uplift readers and make a lasting impact on their lives.

- Phanuel Ochieng'.

Preface

Dear Reader,

I never thought I would write a book, let alone a memoir. Growing up, I was always shy and introverted, preferring to keep my thoughts and feelings to myself. But as I grew older and began to face the challenges and complexities of life, I found solace in writing. I began to keep a diary, documenting my experiences, thoughts, and emotions as a way of processing and making sense of the world around me.

Over time, my diary became a trusted companion, a safe space where I could be my truest self without fear of judgment. It was a place where I could reflect on my experiences and explore my hopes and dreams for the future.

As I approached adulthood, I realized that my diary was more than just a personal record - it was a testament to my growth and resilience. It was a chronicle of my journey through life, with all its twists and turns, highs and lows.

And so, I decided to share my journey with the world. "Dear Diary. The Journey" is a collection of diary entries, reflections, and insights that I have gathered over the years. It is a story of self-discovery, of finding one's place in the world, and of learning to embrace the journey with all its joys and challenges.

I hope that this book will serve as a source of inspiration and encouragement to all those who read it. May it remind you that, no matter what life may throw your way, you are capable of overcoming adversity and achieving your dreams.

Thank you for embarking on this journey with me.

Sincerely,

Prince Sammysam.

Acknowledgements

I would like to express my heartfelt gratitude to the following individuals and organizations who have supported me throughout my writing journey:

To my family, for their unwavering love and support. Your encouragement and belief in me have been my anchor, and I am forever grateful for the sacrifices you have made to help me pursue my dreams.

To my mom, Ruth Achieng', for being a constant source of inspiration and guidance. Your wisdom and strength have taught me to persevere through life's challenges and to always stay true to my values.

To my siblings, who I love deeply, for being my biggest cheerleaders and for always being there when I needed them. Your love and support have given me the courage to pursue my passions and to be the best version of myself.

To my friends, for their unwavering support and encouragement throughout my writing journey. Your belief in me and your willingness to listen and offer advice have been invaluable, and I am blessed to have you in my life.

Finally, I would like to express my gratitude to my publishers, Pencil, for their belief in me and for providing me with the opportunity to share my story with the world. Your professionalism, expertise, and guidance have been instrumental in bringing this book to fruition.

Thank you to everyone who has supported me along the way. Your kindness and generosity have meant the world to me, and I am blessed to have you in my life.

Introduction

Have you ever kept a diary? Have you ever poured your heart and soul onto the pages of a journal, documenting your deepest thoughts and feelings? If so, then you know the power of writing to heal, to inspire, and to transform.

For as long as I can remember, I have been a writer. As a child, I would scribble stories and poems in notebooks, imagining worlds beyond my small town. As I grew older, my writing became more personal, more introspective. I began to keep a diary, recording my daily experiences, hopes, and fears.

At first, my diary was just a hobby - something I did to pass the time. But as I grew older and began to face the challenges of adulthood, my diary became a lifeline. It was a place where I could be honest with myself, where I could explore my deepest fears and desires without fear of judgment.

The diary became a companion on my journey through life. It witnessed my triumphs and my failures, my joys and my sorrows. It was a constant source of comfort and support, reminding me that I was never truly alone.

And now, I am ready to share my journey with you. "Dear Diary. The Journey" is a collection of diary entries, reflections, and insights that I have gathered over the years. It is a testament to the power of writing to heal, to inspire, and to transform.

In this book, you will find a story of resilience, of hope, and of the human spirit's capacity to endure and flourish in the face of adversity. It is a story of the universal human experience - of love, loss, family, and the search for meaning and purpose.

I invite you to join me on this journey, to open yourself up to the possibilities that life has to offer, and to embrace the power of writing to transform your own life.

Sincerely,

Prince Sammysam

Reflection.

The Journey Within"

The journey within, is a journey so deep,
A journey of reflection, that's ours to keep.
For in the world of introspection,
We find a beauty, that's like no other.

With each new thought, a new chance to see,
The beauty of life, and all that it can be.
For reflection is a journey, of self-discovery,
And in its twists and turns, we find our glory.

So let us embrace, the power of reflection,
And let our hearts, be filled with love and affection.
For in our reflections, we find our way,
To a brighter tomorrow, and a better day.

"Life's Lessons"

Life's lessons, are lessons so dear,
A chance to learn, and conquer our fear.
For in the world of lessons learned,
We find a beauty, that's like no other.

With each new experience, a new chance to see,
The beauty of life, and all that it can be.
For life's lessons are a journey, of self-discovery,
And in its twists and turns, we find our glory.

So let us embrace, the power of life's lessons,
And let our hearts, be filled with love and blessings.
For in our reflections, we find our way,
To a brighter tomorrow, and a better day.

"The Meaning of Life"

The meaning of life, is a question so deep,
A question of purpose, that's ours to keep.
For in the world of searching for meaning,
We find a beauty, that's like no other.

With each new idea, a new chance to see,
The beauty of life, and all that it can be.
For finding meaning is a journey, of self-discovery,
And in its twists and turns, we find our glory.

So let us embrace, the question of meaning,
And let our hearts, be filled with love and leaning.
For in our reflections, we find our way,
To a brighter tomorrow, and a better day.

"The Passage of Time"

The passage of time, is a thing so dear,
A chance to grow, and conquer our fear.
For in the world of time's passing,

We find a beauty, that's like no other.

With each new day, a new chance to see,
The beauty of life, and all that it can be.
For time's passage is a journey, of self-discovery,
And in its twists and turns, we find our glory.

So let us embrace, the power of time's passage,
And let our hearts, be filled with love and courage.
For in our reflections, we find our way,
To a brighter tomorrow, and a better day.

"The Complexity of Existence"

The complexity of existence, is a thing so vast,
A chance to explore, and make it last.
For in the world of existence's questions,
We find a beauty, that's like no other.

With each new thought, a new chance to see,
The beauty of life, and all that it can be.
For existence's complexity is a journey, of self-discovery,
And in its twists and turns, we find our glory.

So let us embrace, the complexity of existence,
And let our hearts, be filled with love and persistence.
For in our reflections, we find our way,
To a brighter tomorrow, and a better day.

The Power of Reflection"

The power of reflection, is a power so strong,
A chance to reflect, and see where we belong.
For in the world of reflection's insight,
We find a beauty, that's like no other.

With each new thought, a new chance to see,
The beauty of life, and all that it can be.
For reflection's power is a journey, of self-discovery,
And in its twists and turns, we find our glory.

So let us embrace, the power of reflection,
And let our hearts, be filled with love and affection.
For in our reflections, we find our way,
To a brighter tomorrow, and a better day.

Early Years.

The Journey Within"

The journey within, is a journey so deep,
A journey of reflection, that's ours to keep.
For in the world of introspection,
We find a beauty, that's like no other.

With each new thought, a new chance to see,
The beauty of life, and all that it can be.
For reflection is a journey, of self-discovery,
And in its twists and turns, we find our glory.

So let us embrace, the power of reflection,
And let our hearts, be filled with love and affection.
For in our reflections, we find our way,
To a brighter tomorrow, and a better day.

"Life's Lessons"

Life's lessons, are lessons so dear,
A chance to learn, and conquer our fear.
For in the world of lessons learned,
We find a beauty, that's like no other.

With each new experience, a new chance to see,
The beauty of life, and all that it can be.
For life's lessons are a journey, of self-discovery,
And in its twists and turns, we find our glory.

So let us embrace, the power of life's lessons,
And let our hearts, be filled with love and blessings.
For in our reflections, we find our way,
To a brighter tomorrow, and a better day.

"The Meaning of Life"

The meaning of life, is a question so deep,
A question of purpose, that's ours to keep.
For in the world of searching for meaning,
We find a beauty, that's like no other.

With each new idea, a new chance to see,
The beauty of life, and all that it can be.
For finding meaning is a journey, of self-discovery,
And in its twists and turns, we find our glory.

So let us embrace, the question of meaning,
And let our hearts, be filled with love and leaning.
For in our reflections, we find our way,
To a brighter tomorrow, and a better day.

"The Passage of Time"

The passage of time, is a thing so dear,
A chance to grow, and conquer our fear.
For in the world of time's passing,

We find a beauty, that's like no other.

With each new day, a new chance to see,
The beauty of life, and all that it can be.
For time's passage is a journey, of self-discovery,
And in its twists and turns, we find our glory.

So let us embrace, the power of time's passage,
And let our hearts, be filled with love and courage.
For in our reflections, we find our way,
To a brighter tomorrow, and a better day.

"The Complexity of Existence"

The complexity of existence, is a thing so vast,
A chance to explore, and make it last.
For in the world of existence's questions,
We find a beauty, that's like no other.

With each new thought, a new chance to see,
The beauty of life, and all that it can be.
For existence's complexity is a journey, of self-discovery,
And in its twists and turns, we find our glory.

So let us embrace, the complexity of existence,
And let our hearts, be filled with love and persistence.
For in our reflections, we find our way,
To a brighter tomorrow, and a better day.

The Power of Reflection"

The power of reflection, is a power so strong,
A chance to reflect, and see where we belong.
For in the world of reflection's insight,
We find a beauty, that's like no other.

With each new thought, a new chance to see,
The beauty of life, and all that it can be.
For reflection's power is a journey, of self-discovery,
And in its twists and turns, we find our glory.

So let us embrace, the power of reflection,
And let our hearts, be filled with love and affection.
For in our reflections, we find our way,
To a brighter tomorrow, and a better day.

Creativity.

"The Muse Within"

The muse within, is a thing so grand,
A chance to create, and take a stand.
For in the world of personal expression,
We find a beauty, that's like no other.

With each new idea, a new chance to see,
The beauty of life, and all that it can be.
For creativity is a journey, of self-discovery,
And in its twists and turns, we find our glory.

So let us embrace, the muse within,
And let our hearts, be filled with love and spin.
For in our creativity, we find our way,
To a brighter tomorrow, and a better day.

The Power of Expression"

The power of expression, is a power so strong,
A chance to create, and sing a song.
For in the world of personal creativity,
We find a beauty, that's like no other.

With each new stroke, a new chance to be,
A part of the world, and all that it can be.
For personal expression is a journey, of self-discovery,
And in its twists and turns, we find our glory.

So let us embrace, the power of expression,
And let our hearts, be filled with love and impression.
For in our creativity, we find our way,
To a brighter tomorrow, and a better day.

The Joy of Creation"

The joy of creation, is a joy so sweet,
A chance to create, and make things complete.
For in the world of personal creativity,
We find a beauty, that's like no other.

With each new creation, a new chance to see,
The beauty of life, and all that it can be.
For the joy of creation is a journey, of self-discovery,
And in its twists and turns, we find our glory.

So let us embrace, the joy of creation,
And let our hearts, be filled with love and elation.
For in our creativity, we find our way,
To a brighter tomorrow, and a better day.

"The Freedom of Creativity"

The freedom of creativity, is a freedom so rare,
A chance to create, and show that we care.
For in the world of personal expression,

We find a beauty, that's like no other.

With each new creation, a new chance to be,
A part of the world, and all that it can be.
For the freedom of creativity is a journey, of self-discovery,
And in its twists and turns, we find our glory.

So let us embrace, the freedom of creativity,
And let our hearts, be filled with love and activity.
For in our creativity, we find our way,
To a brighter tomorrow, and a better day.

Family Matters and The Power of Writing.

Family Matters

Family, a bond that runs so deep,
A love that never fades or sleeps.
Through thick and thin, they're by your side,
A comfort and a source of pride.

But families, too, can face their strife,
Their own unique struggles in this life.
A loss, a change, a conflict brews,
A test of strength, of love, of truths.

It was during these trying times,
That my family faced its own uphill climb.
The pain was raw, the wounds so deep,
A journey we had to take, to keep.

We faced our demons, we shed our tears,
We held each other, through all our fears.
And in the end, we found our way,
Closer, stronger, day by day.

For family, a bond that runs so deep,
Can weather any storm, and rise to meet,
The challenges that life may bring,

And come out stronger, with love that sings.

So here's to family, and all they bring,
A source of love and hope, that never dims.

****

The Power of Writing

Words, like magic, on the page,
A power to heal, to inspire, to engage.
Through pen and paper, a story unfolds,
A window to the soul, a tale to be told.

It was through writing, that I found my way,
Through the ups and downs, the light and the gray.
My diary, a friend, a confidante true,
A place to be myself, to start anew.

Through writing, I found my voice,
A way to express, to make a choice.
To face my fears, to chase my dreams,
To explore my world, or so it seems.

And as I wrote, the world came alive,
A canvas of stories, of hopes and of strife.
Through characters and plots, I found my way,
To a life of purpose, to a brighter day.

So here's to writing, and all its might,
A power to heal, to inspire, to ignite.
May we all find our voice, our story to tell,
And through our words, may we find our way as well.

Dear diary, I know this journey is going to be a long one,
Please walk it with me, for I have no one else.
With each new step, I'll write my thoughts down,
And let my heart and soul, take flight and delve.

For in these pages, I'll find my voice,
And let my dreams and hopes rejoice.
I'll share my fears, and my deepest pains,
And let my hopes, rise above the strains.

Dear diary, I know you'll be my friend,
Through every twist and turn, until the end.
With each new day, a new story to tell,
Of love and laughter, and moments that swell.

So here's to the journey, that lies ahead,
And the pages we'll fill, with words unsaid.
Dear diary, let's start this journey anew,
And write a story, that's just me and you.

Dear Diary, the journey has been long,
Filled with twists and turns, and a few sad songs.
I've walked through fire, and I've felt the pain,
But with each step, I've learned to rise again.

I've traveled far, and I've seen so much,
From the rolling hills to the ocean's touch.
I've met new people, and I've made some friends,
And I've journeyed through life, from beginning to end.

Dear Diary, the journey's not over yet,
There's still so much left that I haven't met.

But I'll keep on moving, and I'll keep on trying,
With each new step, I'll keep on flying.

I'll take the lessons, and I'll hold them tight,
And I'll keep on moving, through the day and the night.
For the journey's not over, and there's more to come,
And I'll face it head-on, till the journey is done.

So here's to the road, and the path that we take,
And here's to the memories, and the moments we make.
Dear Diary, the journey's been a ride,
But I'm grateful for every step, and every stride.

***

"The Sound of Silence"

The sound of silence fills the air,
A peaceful calm, beyond compare.
In stillness, I find my inner light,
And let my soul take to flight.

The world outside may rage and roar,
But in this moment, I ask for more.
The sound of silence, a sweet refrain,
A chance to breathe, and ease the pain.

In this stillness, I find my peace,
And let my worries and fears release.
The sound of silence, a calming balm,
A chance to rest, and be reborn.

For in this moment, I'm free to be,
To let my heart and soul run free.
The sound of silence, a moment divine,
A chance to connect, with the divine.

So let the world outside rage and roar,
For in this moment, I ask for more.
The sound of silence, a sweet refrain,
A chance to breathe, and ease the pain.

"The Colors of Life"

Life is a canvas, painted bright,
With colors bold, and hues of light.
Each stroke a moment, each shade a dream,
A tapestry woven, with each new theme.

From the darkest black, to the brightest white,
The colors of life, are a beautiful sight.
With each new day, a new palette to see,
A chance to paint, our own destiny.

In the colors of life, we find our way,
Through the ups and downs, and the day to day.
For life is a canvas, with no set plan,
A chance to create, our own wonderland.

With each new stroke, a new story to tell,
Of love and laughter, and overcoming hell.
For the colors of life, are a reflection true,
Of all we've been, and all we do.

So let us paint, with colors bright,
And let our dreams take to the light.
For life is a canvas, painted with love,
A chance to soar, like a dove.

"The Whisper of the Wind"

The whisper of the wind, so soft and light,
A fleeting moment, in the still of night.
It carries with it, secrets untold,
And stories of love, from days of old.

With each new breeze, a new tale to hear,
A chance to listen, with an open ear.
For the whisper of the wind, is a voice so true,
And in its gentle embrace, we find something new.

Through the rustling leaves, and the bending trees,
The whisper of the wind, carries with it, a breeze.
A chance to connect, with nature's soul,
And feel the peace, that makes us whole.

For in the whisper of the wind, we hear a call,
To let go of the worries, and let our spirits fall.
To feel the power, of the earth and sky,
And let our souls, take to the high.

So let the whisper of the wind, guide us true,
And let its gentle caress, carry us through.
For in its soft embrace, we find our way,
To a brighter tomorrow, and a better day.

Personal Growth.

"A Journey of Self-Discovery"

Life is a journey, we all must take,
With twists and turns, and paths to make.
Along the way, we find our way,
And learn to grow, from day to day.

Through hardships, we find our strength,
And learn to rise, above the length.
For in our struggles, we find our light,
And learn to shine, with all our might.

With each new step, a new lesson learned,
And with each new turn, a new page turned.
For life is a journey, of self-discovery,
And in its twists and turns, we find our glory.

So let us embrace, the journey we're on,
And let our hearts, carry us along.
For in our personal growth, we find our way,
To a brighter tomorrow, and a better day.

"The Power of Change"

Change is the only constant, they say,
And in our personal growth, we find our way.
For in the changes we make, we find our strength,
And learn to rise, above the length.

Through the trials and tribulations, we find our light,
And learn to shine, with all our might.
For in our personal growth, we find our power,
And learn to face, each new hour.

With each new change, a new chapter begins,
And with each new step, a new story begins.
For life is a journey, of self-discovery,
And in its twists and turns, we find our glory.

So let us embrace, the power of change,
And let our hearts, carry us through the range.
For in our personal growth, we find our way,
To a brighter tomorrow, and a better day.

"The Road to Self-Acceptance"

The road to self-acceptance, is a journey long,
With ups and downs, and rights and wrongs.
But with each new step, we learn to love,
And let our hearts, rise above.

Through the doubts and fears, we find our voice,
And learn to make, the right choice.
For in our personal growth, we find our way,
And learn to shine, with all our might each day.

With each new obstacle, a new lesson learned,
And with each new turn, a new page turned.
For life is a journey, of self-discovery,
And in its twists and turns, we find our glory.

So let us embrace, the road to self-acceptance,
And let our hearts, carry us through the distance.
For in our personal growth, we find our power,
And learn to face, each new hour.

"The Art of Letting Go"

The art of letting go, is a lesson hard,
But in our personal growth, we find our regard.
For in the moments we release, we find our peace,
And let our hearts, rise above the crease.

Through the pain and sorrow, we find our truth,
And learn to let go, of the youth.
For in our personal growth, we find our way,
And learn to make, a brighter day.

With each new memory, a new moment to hold,
And with each new page, a new story told.
For life is a journey, of self-discovery,
And in its twists and turns, we find our glory.

So let us embrace, the art of letting go,
And let our hearts, carry us through the flow.
For in our personal growth, we find our power,
And learn to face, each new hour.

"The Courage to Be Yourself"

The courage to be yourself, is a journey long,
With fears and doubts, and rights and wrongs.
But with each new step, we find our way,
And learn to shine, with all our might each day.

Through the judgments and criticisms, we find our voice,
And learn to make, the right choice.
For in our personal growth, we find our power,
And learn to face, each new hour.

With each new expression, a new piece of art,
And with each new start, a new chance to restart.
For life is a journey, of self-discovery,
And in its twists and turns, we find our glory.

So let us embrace, the courage to be ourselves,
And let our hearts, carry us through the delves.
For in our personal growth, we find our way,
To a brighter tomorrow, and a better day.

******

I'm glad you found the poems inspiring! There are many great books on personal growth that can help you deepen your understanding of yourself and the world around you. Here are a few recommendations:

1. "The Power of Now" by Eckhart Tolle: This book offers practical guidance on how to live in the present

moment and cultivate a deeper sense of awareness and inner peace.

2. "Man's Search for Meaning" by Viktor Frankl: This book explores the human search for meaning and purpose, drawing on the author's experiences as a Holocaust survivor and psychotherapist.

3. "The Alchemist" by Paulo Coelho: This novel tells the story of a shepherd boy on a journey of self-discovery and spiritual awakening, and offers insights into the nature of courage, faith, and destiny.

4. "The Four Agreements" by Don Miguel Ruiz: This book offers a set of principles for living a fulfilling and authentic life, based on the ancient wisdom of the Toltec people of Mexico.

5. "Daring Greatly" by Brené Brown: This book explores the importance of vulnerability, courage, and authenticity in cultivating meaningful relationships and living a fulfilling life.

I hope you find them helpful on your own journey of self-discovery!

Relationships,Heartbreak and Healing.

"Broken Pieces"

I was shattered, like pieces of glass,
My heart was broken, and I couldn't go back.
I cried and screamed, but no one could hear,
The pain I felt, was so severe.

But slowly, I picked up the pieces,
And tried to mend what was left of me.
I learned to let go of the pain,
And open my heart, to love again.

For in the broken pieces, I found my strength,
And learned to rise, above the length.
And in my healing, I found my peace,
And let my heart, rise above the creas.

The Art of Healing"

Healing is an art, they say,
And in my heartbreak, I found my way.
For in the pain and sorrow, I found my light,
And learned to shine, with all my might.

Through the tears and anguish, I found my voice,
And learned to make, the right choice.
For in my healing, I found my power,
And learned to face, each new hour.

With each new day, a new chance to heal,
And with each new turn, a new chance to feel.
For healing is a journey, of self-discovery,
And in its twists and turns, we find our glory.

So let us embrace, the art of healing,
And let our hearts, carry us through the feeling.
For in our healing, we find our way,
To a brighter tomorrow, and a better day.

The Strength Within"

I thought I was weak, when you left me behind,
My heart was shattered, and I lost my mind.
But deep within, a strength arose,
And I learned to let go, of my woes.

For in the pain and heartbreak, I found my voice,
And learned to make, the right choice.
I learned to love, and trust again,
And let my heart, rise above the pain.

With each new step, a new lesson learned,
And with each new turn, a new page turned.
For healing is a journey, of self-discovery,
And in its twists and turns, we find our glory.

So let us embrace, the strength within,
And let our hearts, carry us through the spin.
For in our healing, we find our way,
To a brighter tomorrow, and a better day.

The Road to Recovery"

The road to recovery, is a journey long,
With ups and downs, and rights and wrongs.
But with each new step, we find our way,
And learn to shine, with all our might each day.

Through the pain and heartbreak, we find our truth,
And learn to let go, of the youth.
For in our recovery, we find our power,
And learn to face, each new hour.

With each new memory, a new moment to hold,
And with each new page, a new story told.
For recovery is a journey, of self-discovery,
And in its twists and turns, we find our glory.

So let us embrace, the road to recovery,
And let our hearts, carry us through the discovery.
For in our healing, we find our way,
To a brighter tomorrow, and a better day.

The Beauty in the Break"

There's beauty in the break, they say,
And in my heartbreak, I found my way.

For in the pain and sorrow, I found my light,
And learned to shine, with all my might.

Through the tears and anguish, I found my voice,
And learned to make, the right choice.
For in my healing, I found my power,
And learned to face, each new hour.

With each new day, a new chance to grow,
And with each new turn, a new chance to know.
For healing is a journey, of self-discovery,
And in its twists and turns, we find our glory.

So let us embrace, the beauty in the break,
And let our hearts, carry us through the ache.
For in our healing, we find our way,
To a brighter tomorrow, and a better day.

The Gift of Healing"

Healing is a gift, they say,
And in my heartbreak, I found my way.
For in the pain and sorrow, I found my light,
And learned to shine, with all my might.

Through the tears and anguish, I found my voice,
And learned to make, the right choice.
For in my healing, I found my power,
And learned to face, each new hour.

With each new moment, a new chance to heal,
And with each new turn, a new chance to feel.
For healing is a journey, of self-discovery,
And in its twists and turns, we find our glory.

So let us embrace, the gift of healing,
And let our hearts, carry us through the feeling.
For in our healing, we find our way,
To a brighter tomorrow, and a better day.

The Wings of Healing"

In my heartbreak, my wings were broken,
And I couldn't fly, with words unspoken.
But then I found, the wings of healing,
And learned to fly, with a new feeling.

For in the pain and sorrow, I found my truth,
And learned to let go, of the youth.
I learned to love, and trust again,
And let my heart, rise above the pain.

With each new step, a new lesson learned,
And with each new turn, a new page turned.
For healing is a journey, of self-discovery,
And in its twists and turns, we find our glory.

So let us embrace, the wings of healing,
And let our hearts, carry us through the feeling.
For in ourhealing, we find our way,
To a brighter tomorrow, and a better day.

****

I'm glad you enjoyed the poems! Here are a few book recommendations on healing from heartbreak:

1. "How to Fix a Broken Heart" by Guy Winch: This book offers practical advice on how to heal from heartbreak, including strategies for dealing with emotional pain and rebuilding self-esteem.

2. "The Breakup Bible" by Rachel Sussman: This book offers a step-by-step guide to healing from a breakup, including tips for coping with difficult emotions, finding support, and moving on in a healthy way.

3. "It's Called a Breakup Because It's Broken" by Greg Behrendt and Amiira Ruotola-Behrendt: This book offers humor and compassion as it guides readers through the process of healing from a breakup, including advice on how to let go of the past and embrace the future.

4. "The Wisdom of a Broken Heart" by Susan Piver: This book offers a Buddhist-inspired approach to healing from heartbreak, emphasizing the importance of mindfulness, self-compassion, and spiritual growth.

5. "Getting Past Your Breakup" by Susan J. Elliott: This book offers practical advice on how to heal from a breakup, including strategies for dealing with difficult emotions, setting boundaries, and moving on in a healthy way.

I hope you find them helpful on your own journey of healing and growth.

FAMILY
A Bond Unbreakable"

In the arms of family, I found my home,
A bond unbreakable, no matter where I roam.
For in their love, I found my strength,
And in their care, I found my length.

Through the ups and downs, they stood by my side,
And in their love, I found my guide.
For in our journey, we found our way,
To a brighter tomorrow, and a better day.

For family is a gift, beyond compare,
A love so pure, and so rare.
And in their embrace, I found my peace,
And let my heart, rise above the crease.

A Circle of Love"

In the circle of family, I found my joy,
A love so pure, and so coy.
For in their laughter, I found my light,
And in their embrace, I found my might.

Through the years, we grew together,
And in our journey, we found our weather.
For in the storms, we held on tight,
And in the sunshine, we took flight.

For family is a circle, of love and care,
A bond so strong, and so rare.
And in their embrace, I found my home,
A love unbreakable, no matter where I roam.

The Gift of Family"

In the gift of family, I found my way,
A love so deep, and so gay.
For in their wisdom, I found my truth,
And in their care, I found my youth.

Through the trials and tribulations, we stood strong,
And in our love, we found our song.
For in our journey, we found our might,
And in our bond, we found our light.

For family is a gift, beyond compare,
A love so pure, and so rare.
And in their embrace, I found my peace,
And let my heart, rise above the crease.

The Power of Family"

In the power of family, I found my way,
A love so strong, and so gay.
For in their courage, I found my strength,
And in their care, I found my length.

Through the twists and turns, we held on tight,
And in our journey, we found our light.
For in our love, we found our power,

And in our bond, we found our tower.

For family is a power, beyond compare,
A love so pure, and so rare.
And in their embrace, I found my home,
A love unbreakable, no matter where I roam.

The Heart of Family"

In the heart of family, I found my peace,
A love so pure, and so at ease.
For in their kindness, I found my grace,
And in their care, I found my place.

Through the highs and lows, we stood together,
And in our journey, we found our weather.
For in our bond, we found our light,
And in our love, we found our might.

For family is a heart, beyond compare,
A love so pure, and so rare.
And in their embrace, I found my home,
A love unbreakable, no matter where I roam.

Challenges.

A Life of Challenges"

Life is full of challenges, that much is true,
And I've faced my fair share, more than a few.
From poverty and struggle, to loss and pain,
I've weathered the storm, again and again.

But through it all, I've found my strength,
And learned to rise, above the length.
For in my challenges, I found my power,
And learned to face, each new hour.

With each new obstacle, a new chance to grow,
And with each new challenge, a new chance to know.
For life is a journey, of self-discovery,
And in its twists and turns, we find our glory.

So let us embrace, the challenges we face,
And let our hearts, carry us through the race.
For in our journey, we find our way,
To a brighter tomorrow, and a better day.

The Pain of Loss"

The pain of loss, is a heavy weight,
A burden we carry, both early and late.
For when we lose, someone we love,
Our hearts are broken, and we can't rise above.

But slowly, we learn to let go,
And find a way, to heal and grow.
For in our memories, they live on,
And in our hearts, they shine like the dawn.

With each new day, a new chance to heal,
And with each new turn, a new chance to feel.
For healing is a journey, of self-discovery,
And in its twists and turns, we find our glory.

So let us embrace, the pain of loss,
And let our hearts, carry us across.
For in our journey, we find our way,
To a brighter tomorrow, and a better day.

The Struggle of Poverty"

The struggle of poverty, is a heavy load,
A burden we carry, down life's winding road.
For when we lack, the basic needs of life,
Our hearts are heavy, and we can't rise above.

But slowly, we learn to make do,
And find a way, to see it through.
For in our struggle, we find our strength,
And learn to rise, above the length.

With each new challenge, a new chance to grow,
And with each new obstacle, a new chance to know.
For life is a journey, of self-discovery,
And in its twists and turns, we find our glory.

So let us embrace, the struggle of poverty,
And let our hearts, carry us through the adversity.
For in our journey, we find our way,
To a brighter tomorrow, and a better day.

The Light of Hope"

In the darkest of days, there is a light,
A spark of hope, shining so bright.
For even in our struggles, we can find,
A way to rise, and leave it all behind.

Through the pain and sorrow, we can see,
A brighter tomorrow, waiting for you and me.
For hope is a beacon, shining so true,
A light in the darkness, guiding us through.

With each new step, a new chance to believe,
And with each new turn, a new chance to achieve.
For hope is a journey, of self-discovery,
And in its twists and turns, we find our glory.

So let us embrace, the light of hope,
And let our hearts, carry us through the slope.
For in our journey, we find our way,
To a brighter tomorrow, and a better day.

The Strength Within"

In the struggles of life, we find our way,
A strength within, shining so gay.
For even in our darkest hour,
We can find the strength, and rise with power.

Through the pain and heartbreak, we can see,
A way to heal, and set ourselves free.
For strength is a gift, that lies within,
A power to rise, and start again.

With each new challenge, a new chance to grow,
And with each new obstacle, a new chance to know.
For life is a journey, of self-discovery,
And in its twists and turns, we find our glory.

So let us embrace, the strength within,
And let our hearts, carry us through the spin.
For in our journey, we find our way,
To a brighter tomorrow, and a better day.

The Journey"

Life is a journey, with twists and turns,
A path we follow, as our heart yearns.
For even in our struggles, we can find,
A way to rise, and leave it all behind.

Through the pain and sorrow, we can see,
A brighter tomorrow, waiting for you and me.
For life is a journey, of self-discovery,

A chance to grow, and find our glory.

With each new step, a new chance to learn,
And with each new turn,a new chance to earn
A life full of love, and joy, and peace,
A life that's full, and free, and at ease.

For in our journey, we find our way,
And in our struggles, we find our play.
For life is a gift, beyond compare,
A journey we take, with love and care.

So let us embrace, the journey we're on,
And let our hearts, carry us along.
For in our journey, we find our way,
To a brighter tomorrow, and a better day.

The Journey Begins"

The journey begins, with a single step,
A dream in our hearts, that we can't forget.
For even in our struggles, we can find,
A way to rise, and leave it all behind.

With each new day, a new chance to grow,
And with each new turn, a new chance to know.
For life is a journey, of self-discovery,
And in its twists and turns, we find our glory.

So let us embrace, the journey ahead,
And let our hearts, be our guide and stead.
For in our journey, we find our way,

To a brighter tomorrow, and a better day.

The Power of Persistence"

The power of persistence, is a force so strong,
A will to keep going, even when things go wrong.
For even in our struggles, we can find,
A way to rise, and leave it all behind.

With each new setback, a new chance to learn,
And with each new challenge, a new chance to earn
Our place in the world, and make our mark,
And shine our light, even in the dark.

For the journey is long, but we're not alone,
We have our dreams, and our hearts to own.
For in our journey, we find our way,
To a brighter tomorrow, and a better day.

The Courage to Believe"

The courage to believe, is a gift so rare,
A faith in ourselves, that we can't compare.
For even in our struggles, we can find,
A way to rise, and leave it all behind.

With each new doubt, a new chance to trust,
And with each small step, a new chance to adjust.
For courage is a journey, of self-discovery,
And in its twists and turns, we find our glory.

So let us embrace, the courage to believe,
And let our hearts, carry us through the weave.
For in our journey, we find our way,
To a brighter tomorrow, and a better day.

The Journey Continues"

The journey continues, with each passing day,
A new chance to grow, and find our way.
For even when we stumble, we can rise,
And reach for the stars, up in the skies.

With each new challenge, a new chance to learn,
And with each new obstacle, a new chance to earn
Our place in the world, and make our mark,
And shine our light, even in the dark.

For the journey is long, but we're not alone,
We have our dreams, and our hearts to own.
For in our journey, we find our way,
To a brighter tomorrow, and a better day.

Gratitude.

Grateful Heart"

A grateful heart, is a heart at peace,
A soul that's full, and free, and at ease.
For when we count our blessings, one by one,
We realize how far, we have come.

With each new day, a new chance to see,
The beauty in life, and all that it can be.
For gratitude is a journey, of self-discovery,
And in its twists and turns, we find our glory.

So let us embrace, the power of gratitude,
And let our hearts, be filled with a joyful attitude.
For in our journey, we find our way,
To a brighter tomorrow, and a better day.

Thank You"

Thank you for the little things,
The joys that each new day brings.
For the sun that rises, and the stars that shine,
For the love that surrounds us, so divine.

Thank you for the beauty of life,
For the laughter, and the moments of strife.
For the lessons we learn, and the wisdom we gain,
For the love that we share, and the memories we retain.

For in our gratitude, we find our way,
To a brighter tomorrow, and a better day.

Blessings"

Blessings come in all shapes and sizes,
From the smallest things, to the biggest surprises.
For every moment, and every breath we take,
Is a gift to cherish, and not to forsake.

With each new day, a new chance to see,
The blessings that surround us, so free.
For gratitude is a journey, of self-discovery,
And in its twists and turns, we find our glory.

So let us embrace, the blessings of life,
And let our hearts, be free of strife.
For in our journey, we find our way,
To a brighter tomorrow, and a better day.

The Gift of Gratitude"

The gift of gratitude, is a gift so rare,
A treasure we find, beyond compare.
For when we count our blessings, one by one,
We realize how far, we have come.

With each new day, a new chance to grow,
And with each new turn, a new chance to know.
For gratitude is a journey, of self-discovery,
And in its twists and turns, we find our glory.

So let us embrace, the gift of gratitude,
And let our hearts, be filled with a joyful attitude.
For in our journey, we find our way,
To a brighter tomorrow, and a better day.

Gratitude in Action"

Gratitude in action, is a force so strong,
A way to live, that we can't go wrong.
For when we give thanks, and show our love,
We create a world, like the heavens above.

With each new act, a new chance to give,
And with each new step, a new chance to live.
For gratitude is a journey, of self-discovery,
And in its twists and turns, we find our glory.

So let us embrace, gratitude in action,
And let our hearts, be filled with compassion.
For in our journey, we find our way,
To a brighter tomorrow, and a better day.

Appendix

Chapter 6: Lessons Learned
- Reflections on personal growth and development
- Insights on resilience and perseverance
- Gratitude and appreciation for life's journey

Conclusion
Appendix: Diary Entries
Glossary
Acknowledgments

Glossary

- Diary: A book in which one records their personal experiences, thoughts, and feelings on a daily basis.
- Self-discovery: The process of gaining insight into one's own character, emotions, and motivations.
- Resilience: The ability to adapt to and overcome adversity and setbacks.
- Introspection: The act of examining one's own thoughts and feelings.
- Worldview: A person's overall perspective on the world, shaped by their experiences, beliefs, and values.
- Adversity: Difficulties or challenges that one may face in life.
- Empowerment: The process of gaining control and confidence over one's own life and decision making.
- Uplifting: Inspiring or encouraging in a positive way.
- Identity: A person's sense of self, including their personality, beliefs, and values.
- Family: A group of people related by blood, marriage, or adoption who share a common bond and support system.
- Love: A strong feeling of affection, attachment, or devotion towards someone or something.
- Loss: The experience of losing someone or something important or valuable.
- Belief: A conviction or acceptance that something is true or real.

- Strength: A quality or characteristic that gives one the ability to withstand challenges and overcome obstacles.
- Challenges: Difficulties or obstacles that one must face in order to achieve a goal or desired outcome.
- Triumph: A great victory or achievement after overcoming a difficult challenge or obstacle.

www.ingramcontent.com/pod-product-compliance
Lightning Source LLC
Chambersburg PA
CBHW060226170726
48004CB00004BA/1453